I0483949

Fibonacci Retracement : Simplified

Profitable Trading Method for
Forex Intraday Trading

Written by

Sankar Srinivasan

LEOPARD BOOKS .COM

Sankar Srinivasan

National Stock Exchange of India's
Certified Market Professional & Technical Analyst

Prepared for Publication by

V.S. PAUL DANIEL ARAVINTH
pauldanielaravinth@gmail.com
(With permission of my father Sankar Srinivasan)

Published by:

LEOPARD BOOKS INDIA
http://LeoPardBooks.com

© Sankar Srinivasan
All rights reserved

ISBN-10: 1508932727
ISBN-13: 978-1508932727

Printed by **CreateSpace**, an *Amazon.com* Company

Our Print Books and E-Books are available at
http://amazon.com and all Amazon sites,
http://LeoPardBooks.com, Kobo, Smashwords, Nook Barnes
& Noble, ScribD, Apple and all leading International online
book stores & E-Book stores

Search Terms: "Sankar Srinivasan"

© Sankar Srinivasan
All rights reserved

Print Book Edition, License Notes

This book is licensed for your personal reading only. This book may not be re-sold or given away to other people. If you would like to share this book with another person, please purchase an additional copy for each recipient. If you're reading this book and did not purchased it, or it was not purchased for your use only, then please return to author, purchase your own copy. Thank you for respecting the hard work of this author.

Table of Contents

About Leonardo Fibonacci 5

Fibonacci Retracement 10

Fibonacci Retracement Calculations 13

HOW IT WORKS IN STOCK MARKET??? 16

ESSENTIAL QUALIFICATIONS FOR TRADING...25

WHEN A MAN's TREND CHANGES 31

About Author 41

About Leonardo Fibonacci

Who was Fibonacci?

Leonardo Fibonacci Pisano, was Italian mathematician born in Pisa during the The middle Ages. He was renowned as one of the most talented mathematicians of his day. The name Fibonacci itself was a nickname given to Leonardo. It was derived from his grandfather's name and means son of Bonaccio.

While most attribute the Fibonacci sequence to Leonardo, he was not responsible for discovering the sequence. In 1202 Leonardo published a book called, *Liber Abaci*. In it, he derived a method for calculating the growth of the rabbit population.

Suppose a newly-born pair of rabbits, one male, one female, are put in a field. Rabbits are able to mate at the age of one month so that at the end of its second month a female can produce another pair of rabbits. Suppose that our rabbits never die and that the female always produces one new pair (one male, one female) every month from the second month on.

The puzzle that Fibonacci posed was...

How many pairs will there be in one year?

At the end of the first month, they mate, but there is still one only 1 pair.

At the end of the second month the female produces a new pair, so now there are 2 pairs of rabbits in the field.

At the end of the third month, the original female produces a second pair, making 3 pairs in all in the field.

At the end of the fourth month, the original female has produced yet another new pair, the female born two months ago produces her first pair also, making 5 pairs.

This mathematical progression is now recognized as the Fibonacci Sequence. Starting with zero and adding one, each new number in the sequence is the sum of the previous two numbers.

In our example, $0+1 = 1$, $1+1=2$, $1+2=3$, $2+3=5$, and so on.

The sequence of numbers looks like this: 0, 1, 1, 2, 3, 5, 8, 13, 21, 34, 55, 89, 144, 233, to infinity.

From this sequence you can easily reason that at the end of one year there would be 233 pairs of rabbits.

This sequence has repeatedly appeared in popular culture from architecture to music to television. While the series is a powerful tool, the analysis of one number with the number up to four places to the right. The first three are shown below. While some are not exact, if you repeat this mathematical analysis through multiple sets of data, you will see we arrive at some well known and fairly consistent ratios.

21/34 = 0.61764 ~ 0.618 34/21 = 1.61904 ~ 1.619

21/55 = 0.38181 ~ 0.382 55/21 = 2.61904 ~ 2.619

21/89 = 0.23595 ~ 0.236 89/21 = 4.23809 ~ 4.238

The dimensional properties adhering to the 1.618 ratio occur throughout nature and the ratio is most referred to as The Golden Ratio. The uncurling of a fern and the patterns found on various mollusk shells are commonly cited examples of this ratio.

This number, when added to 0.618, equals 1. These ratios have been used for over a hundred years in the financial markets by the likes of W.D. Gann and Ralph Nelson Elliot. Up until the late 90s the tracking and use of these numbers were a manual process.

With the proliferation of real-time charting and data, software that automatically calculated and displayed these levels brought Fibonacci into the financial mainstream.

Fibonacci as a Technical Analysis Tool

While there have been countless books and articles written on the use of Fibonacci in technical analysis, the basics are simple.

On the price scale, these ratios, and several others related to the Fibonacci sequence, often indicate levels at which strong resistance and support will be found. Many times, markets tend to reverse right at levels that coincide with the Fibonacci ratios.

On the time scale Fibonacci ratios are one method of identifying potential market turning points. When Fibonacci levels of price and time coincide you have high probability entry points.

In the next few pages I will talk about how I use the two most common applications of Fibonacci:

• Price Retracements – A strategy for quality entry points

• Price Extensions – An approach to determining how far price will run

Then after we have covered the basics we will talk about bringing it all together and using both Fibonacci Retracements and Fibonacci Extensions at same time and how clustering of these ratios increases the probability of profit.

Fibonacci Retracements:

The Fibonacci Retracement is probably the most heavily used Fibonacci tool in the toolset. You will find Fibonacci Retracements as a solid tool in identifying key support and resistance areas.

If prices have fallen from a recent swing high down to a swing low, the expectation is that price should retrace distance, high to low, by a ratio of the Fibonacci sequence.

In this book, I will show you examples of how potential opportunities when price retraces on and beyond 100% by following another set of Fibonacci ratios:

- 61.8

- 100%

- 161.8%

I use the other primarily as confirmation levels. So let's take a look at some examples of Fibonacci Retracements in use.

Sankar Srinivasan

Fibonacci Retracement

Market tasks of a Trader in Stock, Commodity and Forex Markets

BUY & SELL

Most Traders are BUYing in BEAR market

& SELLing in BULL market

Why this mistakes…..???

Wrong Entry & Exit Areas

Emotional Trades

Trades without any decision, Target

Trades by Rumours

Trades by Tips from someone

Trades Copied from someone

Over Trade

Trading is simple……

When we are able to find correct entry area

When we are able to find correct exit area

When we are able to trade sufficient volume with sufficient margin

How to find exact Entry Area?

With help of Broker Recommendations

Expert Tips

(Both assures Dependability & Expense)

Technical Analysis Software
(Expensive)

So, we need a Theory

We need a theory for a successful trading

Anyone can make new theory for stock market

Or, follow a theory invented by Market Experts

GANN Theory
Fibonacci Theory
Dow Theory
Elliott Wave Theory
and many more…. theories available

WHY WE CHOOSE FIBONACCI THEORY?

Fibonacci Theory is easy to understand

Anyone can use without expert knowledge

We are able to find exact entry and exit areas

We may expect near about 90% Accuracy

Fibonacci was not a stock market person.

No stock trading in his time.

But, his theory is working well even in this modern world.

Fibonacci Retracement Calculations

LEONARDO FIBONACCI

Italian Mathematician, born in Pisa, Italy

Considered as "the most talented Mathematician of the Middle Ages"

No Stock or Commodity markets in his time (1170-1250 AD). But, his mathematical predictions are working well, even today

Fibonacci introduced to Europe, the Hindu-Arabic numeral system primarily through his Composition in 1202 AD.

He also introduced the sequence of numbers (0,1,1,2,3,…………)

Fibonacci became a Guest of Emperor Frederick II, who enjoyed mathematics and science.

In 1240, the Republic of Pisa honoured Fibonacci, by granting him a salary.

FIBONACCI Sequence of Numbers

0,1

Add last 2 numbers, and write 1

0,**1,1**

Add last 2 numbers, and write 2

0,1,**1,2**

Add last 2 numbers, and write 3

0,1,1,**2,3**

Add last 2 numbers, and write 5

0,1,1,2,**3,5**

Add last 2 numbers, and write 8

0,1,1,2,3,**5,8**

Add last 2 numbers, and write 13

0,1,1,2,3,5,**8,13**

Add last 2 numbers, and write 21

0,1,1,2,3,5,8,**13,21**

Add last 2 numbers, and write 34

0,1,1,2,3,5,8,13,21,34… and it goes indefinitely

Then, divide first number by second number, and divide second number by first number

0/1,1/2,3/5,8/13,21/34,…………….

1/0,2/1,5/3,13/8,34/21,…………….

After some steps, you will get 0.618 and 1.618 as answers for all calculations

0 1 1 2 3 5 8 13 21 34

Divide first number by second number

0/1,1/2,3/5,8,13,21/34………

Answers are…

0,1,0.5,0.667,0.6,0.625,0.615,0.618,0.618

Then, divide second number by first number

1/0,2/1,5/3,13/8,34/21…….

Answers are…

1,2,1.5,1.667,1.6,1.618,1.618,1.618…..

So, Fibonacci found that 0.618 and 1.618 is important retracements (steps), in a sequence of numbers.

HOW IT WORKS IN STOCK MARKET???

SIMPLE – If you get High/Low price, assume it is 100%. In this 100%, calculate 61.8% and 161.8% of price. You can find major price change in these areas.

LET US SEE AN EXAMPLE

High Price   – 8000

Low Price   - 7950

Current Price   - 7975

Now, we are going to take trading Decisions, by using Fibonacci Retracement

Step 1 is ……….. High (Minus) Low

$$=8000 - 7950 = 50$$

Step 2

Find BUY area by following Calculations

= Calculate 61.8% of 50

= 50 x 61.8% = 30.90

Add 30.90 with LOW Price

= 30.90 + 7950 = 7980.90

So, BUY AT 7980.90

Step 3

Find First Target Calculation

= Calculate 100% of 50

= 50 x 100% = 50

Add 50 with Low Price

$= 50 + 7950 =$ 8000

So, FIRST TARGET 8000

Like this, Find Second Target

$=$ Calculate 161.8% of 50

$= 50 \times 161.8\% = 80.90$

Add 80.90 with Low Price

$= 80.90 + 7950 = 8030.90$

So, SECOND TARGET 8030.90

Step 4

Find SELL area Calculations

$=$ Calculate 61.8% of 50

$= 50 \times 61.8\% = 30.90$

Less 30.90 from HIGH Price

$= 8000 - 30.90 = 7969.10$

So, SELL AT 7969.10

Step 5

Find First Target by following Calculations

= Calculate 100% of 50

= 50 x 100% = 50

Less 50 from HIGH Price

= 8000-50 = 7950

So, FIRST TARGET 7950

Find Second Target

= Calculate 161.8% of 50

= 50 x 161.8% = 80.90

Less 80.90 from HIGH Price

= 8000-80.90 = 7919.10

So, SECOND TARGET 7919.10

Trading Decision is

BUY AT	7980.90
FIRST TARGET	8000.00
SECOND TARGET	8030.90
OR	
SHORT SELL AT	7969.10
FIRST TARGET	7950.00
SECOND TARGET	7919.10

- For BUY, Low is Stop Loss
- For SELL, High is Stop Loss
- Required data - Day High, Low & Current price
- You can use previous day High & previous day Low for today's overall trade
- Enter the trade BUY or SELL, which one is achieved first
- Use any time of Market

GOLDEN RULES:

- Apply this theory in real time intraday trading in FOREX trading.
- Don't use it for Option trading
- Take Day High, Day Low, Current Price, OR Previous High, Low, Current Price, at ANY POINT OF TIME during market hours
- After calculation, you can find Buy area and Sell area, Targets and Stop Loss
- Use these data for trading.
- If BUY or SELL area achieves, involve trading and close the position
- Use MULTIPLE TIMES per Day per Scrip
- Suggested for Intraday trading only
- All above rules are important. First practice the calculations in virtual trade for few days. Then, you can apply in real time trading.
- When using stop loss, use trailing stop loss

Manual calculation is time consuming. So, please kindly send scan copy or email copy of bill of this book, to **petra.srini@gmail.com**

I will send a excel sheet calculator. In that excel sheet calculator, you just enter high and low price. It will generate entry, target and stop loss within fraction of seconds

- Don't make Early Trade. Wait for 30 to 45 minutes from market opening
- Don't make Over Trade
- Don't Trade without any decision
- Don't Trade with other people's Money
- Don't Trade with Borrowed Money
- Don't appoint another person to trade for you
- Don't invest more than 10%-20% of your Excess Money

ANNEXURE

ESSENTIAL QUALIFICATIONS FOR TRADING

William D. Gann

ESSENTIAL QUALIFICATIONS FOR TRADING

William D. Gann

PATIENCE

Patience is a virtue, especially in the stock market. Acquire it if you can. You must have patience to wait for the right opportunity to come, and not be overanxious and get in too soon. Once you buy or sell a stock and it starts moving in your favor, you must have patience to hold it until there is a good reason or sufficient cause for closing the trade. Never close a trade just because you have a profit; do not become impatient and get out for no real reason.

Every act, either in opening or closing a trade, must have a sound basic cause behind it. Hopes and fears must be eliminated. There is no use selling a stock because you fear it is going down, nor buying it because you hope it is going up. Look at your charts and see which way the trend points and follow it. If no definite trend is shown, use patience and wait.

NERVE

Nerve is just as essential as patience; in fact, nerve is the equal of capital. In getting my experience, I have been broke over 40 times, i. e., I have lost all of my money, but there never has been a time yet when I lost my nerve. Years ago, when I was experimenting and working on methods for forecasting the market, I would get in the market wrong and lose all my working capital, but I never let it get my "goat." I studied very carefully how I made the mistake and what the cause of the loss was. In this way, I profited by every mistake and loss, and was enabled to perfect my method of forecasting and trading so that I could make a success. Looking backward brings nothing but regrets. I always believe in facing the future with nerve and hope. But let the nerve and the hope be based on some sound principle that will prevent costly mistakes of the past.

During my career I have seen many traders who had made one mistake after another and suffered severe losses, and still had some capital to work with but when an opportunity appeared, they lacked the nerve to act. In cases of this kind, the nerve would have been more valuable than capital.

KNOWLEDGE

In the early part of my career I made some great success, and what might be called lucky strikes. I made a lot of money easily and then I spent or lost it easily. But I did not give up or lose my nerve. I always figured that I was a better man after each reverse, because I had acquired experience.

Experience is the only school to learn in and the burnt child is the one who knows the pain from having put his fingers in the fire. Mistakes are all right and hard to avoid. They are good for us, because if we profit by them, they prove valuable. But it is wrong to make the same mistake the second time. Therefore, use every mistake as a stepping stone to progress; analyze each mistake you make and the cause of every loss, in order to avoid repeating the same error in future.

With each experience I had, good or bad, I accumulated knowledge, and after all, knowledge is the greatest power of all, for capital will always come to knowledge. Several years ago a brokerage failure occurred suddenly and unexpectedly, and I lost all of my money. To the ordinary man's way of figuring I was broke, but as a friend of mine expressed it at the time, "He may be without cash, but the knowledge that he has of the stock market is worth hundreds of thousands of dollars and in a short time he will turn that knowledge into cash."

I did come back quickly in a few months' time on a small capital, because I had a greater knowledge of the stock market than ever before, and knowing, by experience, that I had a method based upon mathematical science which could be depended upon to forecast the stock market, I had the nerve to pyramid and press the market hard when my science showed that I was on the right side. What would have been the result had I been without knowledge and only filled with hope? I would have stayed broke, as other traders do who follow the fairy phantom of "hope" in Wall Street trading.

HEALTH AND REST

Good health is essential to success in any line. It is one of the great assets for success in the speculative market. At least twice a year a man should close up all of his trades, get entirely out of the market, and go away for a vacation or stay away from the market and rest up. Let your mind rest and your judgment get clear. The man who continually sticks to any business too long without a rest or change gets his judgment warped. He gets in a rut and sees things from a one-sided point of view.

When you are in the market on either side, it is but human nature for you to hope that it will go your way, and you, therefore, give greater weight to any event that seems to indicate a favorable move to your side. When you are out of the market, you are able to see things as they really are, and judge the market without a distorted view, with hope and fear eliminated. Traders who are continually in the market day in and day out and never allow any time to elapse between trades, sooner or later lose all their money. I know one trader who follows scientific forecasting and makes a success. He never makes more than five or six trades in the year. If he buys stocks during the winter or early spring for a rise, and the advance materializes as he expected, he sells out and takes his profits. Then he leaves the market alone, sometimes for several months. In the summer, if he sees indications of a bull or a bear market starting, he gets in again, and if the market moves his way, he may follow it up and pyramid for several months.

When he gets an indication that the end is near, he closes up his trades, takes his profits, and like the wild geese, wends his way to the sunny South. Sometimes he stays all winter in Florida, hunting and fishing; then goes over to Hot Springs, Arkansas, takes a course of baths; returns to Wall Street in good health and fit for another tilt with the Bulls and Bears.

He makes a specialty of trading in certain favorite stocks. He studies them closely and watches for certain signs that he considers almost infallible. When these signs come, he acts. He does not hurry until the time comes, but when it does, there is no hesitation -- he buys or sells. He keeps cool, calm and collected, and waits for the time to open or close a trade.

Another thing he never does is to expect any fixed amount of profits or set any specific time for getting out. I have often seen him make a trade and it would go against him. He would get out and say, "Well, I guess I'll go back to my office and watch them for awhile." Sometimes it would be days or weeks before he made another trade, but when he did, it was based on some good sound reason, and 90 per cent of the time the second trade proved a winner. But suppose he had held the first trade he made and hoped it would move his way. His judgment, being biased, would have become more unreliable all the time. There is nothing like being out of the market and looking them over from an impartial viewpoint. When there is no definite trend, stay out, watch and wait, and your patience will be rewarded.

W. D. Gann, *Truth of the Stock Tape*

WHEN A MAN's TREND CHANGES

William D. Gann

Man's seasonal trend changes just as the market and he has his good and bad cycles. By keeping a record of your own trades, you can determine when your trend is changing one way or the other. I have been able to make as many as 200 consecutive trades without a loss. When I started the campaign, I did not believe I could make 50 trades without a loss, but I did continue to make perfect trades and close every trade with a profit, until I had made 200 trades. This run of luck or up trend that I was in, had run for some time. If I had no way to forecast it, what sign should I watch to tell when the tide had turned against me and I should get out and wait? The first indication that something was wrong would be the first trade on which I made a loss. I remember that it was a small loss, around $100.

On the next trade I had a loss of over $500. This showed that my trend was changing and turning against me, whether due to bad judgment, ill health, tired nerves, or other causes. If I had been wise, I would have quit and kept all of my profits. I made the third trade and as most traders do, went into the market on a larger scale. This trade soon showed a loss of $5,000 and I did not take the loss quickly. The result was that I continued to make a series of losses until the banks closed in November, 1907, and I could not get any more money out of the banks. I was forced to close out all of my commitments with my brokers and take a big loss, because I was bucking my own trend. My period of good luck had run out, and I was trading in a period which should have been for rest, recreation, and gaining knowledge instead of trying to make more money which I did not need. The banks were unable to pay currency for several months, and I could not get any money to speculate with. I put in my time studying and figuring on the market and found out what caused my mistake and the losses.

I started trading again in the Spring of 1908, and should have had some rule to tell me when my trend had turned in my favor. I began to trade in Wheat and the first three trades I made showed profits. This was a sign that luck was with me and I should press it. I then started a campaign buying Cotton and followed the market right on up, pyramiding at the same time that [legendary trader Jesse] Livermore made his first successful corner in July Cotton. I made a large amount of money.

I could give you many more examples of my experiences of profits and losses but one rule that every trader should watch and follow is, just as soon as he makes two or three wrong trades after a long series of profits, he should quit the market and take a rest. Get away from the market. Allow plenty of time for his judgment to clear up. Then, when he thinks he is right again, make a start on a small trade.

If the first trade goes against him, he should quit again and stay away. Then, when he starts again, if his first two or three trades show profits, he can press his luck and expect a period of success until he sees another sign that the tide has turned against him, when he must again get out of the market.

I have always made the biggest profits after I have remained out of the market for a long period of time and have always made the biggest losses after I have been in a campaign in the market for a long period of time. No man can trade heavily in the market without having a strain on his nervous system, and when his nerves begin to give way and his health is below normal, his judgment gets bad and he begins to make losses.

There is no use in staying in, holding on and hoping, when things start going against you. Take your loss quickly and get out. You will make money by staying out of the market and waiting for an opportunity when the market is right, your physical condition good and your mind at its best. To beat the stock market is a battle of wits. Your mind must be active, keen and alert. You must be able to change your mind and act quickly. When you find that your mind gets sluggish and you cannot act quickly, you are in no position to be in the market. I have been connected with brokerage offices and have known the position of a large number of traders. I have seen the market go against them for days and weeks. Gradually they would start getting out, but a few would be very stubborn and hold on. I call it stubbornness; they called it nerve, but it is not nerve which makes a man hold on when the market is going against him. It is hope and stubbornness. Nerve will not outlast a market that is going against you, and even if the nerve does last, your money will not last to continue to buck the trend. Traders usually talk with each other in the boardroom. When all but two or three have gotten out with losses, they will talk with each other and say they are going to put up more margin, stick it out until the turn comes.

Finally, there is one left, and he will say that he is not going to sell out on the bottom but will see it through. Finally, his hope gives way to despair and he puts in an order to sell at a price on a rally.

The market fails to reach his selling price. Then he changes the price for several days and misses it, and the market continues to go lower. Finally, he gives an order to sell out at the market. That was my signal to buy. I would then buy at the market and invariably made profits. This shows that the *trader nearly always does the wrong thing* at *the wrong time* after he has held on for a long period of time. This proves that the man who has health, money, nerve and knowledge and stays out of the market until the psychological moment can always make big profits.

Some man who has made and lost a lot of money betting on the races wrote the following poem:

>"The time to pitch in is when others discouraged show signs of tire"

>"The battle is fought in the home stretch and won twixt the flag and the wire."

It is the ability to act and begin at a time when others see no hope that helps to make a success in speculation. When everything looks the bluest and nobody can see a ray of hope, it is time to buy good stocks. When the pot is boiling and everybody is optimistic, with not a cloud in the sky, it is time to sell. Hope, in one case, has wrecked and ruined judgment and, at the other extreme, fear has caused loss of hope, loss of judgment, and through discouragement, traders sell out on the bottom and many of them go short. This is the wise fool's opportunity and the man who has nerve to weighed in at these extremes will make money.

The man with money who is out of the market and is studying and watching his charts can see these opportunities at the extremes and take advantage of them.

FEAR Vs KNOWLEDGE

Fear is one of the great causes of losses in Wall Street. In fact, fear is the cause of most all of our troubles and misfortunes in life. What causes fear? It is ignorance or lack of knowledge. The Bible says, "Ye shall know the truth and the truth shall make you free." The truth is knowledge whether it is scientific or otherwise, and when a man has knowledge, he sees and knows and does not fear.

With knowledge, he does not hope, because he knows what will happen, and does not hope or fear what will happen.

Why does a man sell out stocks at the lowest point? It is because he fears they will go lower. If he knew that they were at the lowest point, he would have no fear, and instead of selling, he would buy. The same applies at the top. Why does a man buy at the highest point or cover shorts at the highest point? Because he has lost hope and fears they are going higher. If he had knowledge, he would have no fear and would use good judgment. To succeed, hope and fear must be eliminated, and the only way to eliminate these two imposters is to get as much knowledge as you can.

WHY TRADERS DO NOT SELL OUT STOCKS AT HIGH LEVELS

In every bull market many traders have enormous profits, but fail to get out at the right time. They let stocks decline and sometimes wipe out 50 to 100 points' profit before selling out. There must be a reason for this. We have heard much talk of Wall Street psychology and some writers have said that the 1929 Wall Street panic was due to mob psychology. This is largely true, but mob psychology would not have caused the panic if previously mob psychology had not caused the big bull market when everybody bought, got over-optimistic and failed to get out with big profits.

The following incident, which actually happened, illustrates why people do not sell out stocks when they have big profits. A gentleman who I have known for many years bought U. S. Steel around 80 in 1921. He held it and received the stock dividend of 40 per cent in 1927. Then, when the new stock declined to 111 1/4, he bought some when it rallied to 115, and held all of this stock until it advanced to 261 3/4 in September, 1929.

Long before the stock crossed 175, he talked about selling it at 200, but when it crossed 200, he decided that it was going to 250, and waited to sell at that price. About the time that U. S. Steel advanced to 250 this man met a friend of mine and said to him, "What does Gann think of Steel now?"

My friend replied, "Gann says that the market is going to be top around the end of August and he is going to go short of U. S. Steel."

This man said, "I hear that U. S. Steel is going to 300 or higher and then be split up 4 for 1, and then I am going to sell out."

After U. S. Steel sold at 150 in November, 1929, this man came into the office of my friend who said to him, "Mr. H., did you sell your U. S. Steel above $250?"

He answered, "No, I did not sell it, and I have it yet."

My friend said, "Why on earth didn't you sell out when you had such big profits?"

The man replied, "Well, you know they have a way of hypnotizing you and putting you to sleep when stocks are up near top, then you don't wake up and realize what has happened until they are down near the bottom and it is too late to sell."

This man's statement shows that people do get hypnotized and do not realize what has happened or what is going to happen until it is too late, which is one of the reasons why they do not sell out stocks at high levels. If investors and traders would only learn to follow up their profits with a stop loss order, which would get them out with a good part of their profits when the decline starts, they would be much better off.

What was the use of this man allowing U. S. Steel, which he had bought at the right time, to decline over 100 points and wipe out the biggest part of his profits? Of course, after Steel was down 20 points he did not believe that it would decline 80 or 90 points more; if he had, he would have sold out. Remember, it is not what you believe, think or hope that counts, but it is what the market does, therefore you must have some rule to protect your profits, once you have made them. I know of no better automatic protection than the stop loss order.

THE WISE FOOL

The cock-sure trader, who thinks he knows it all, follows tips and inside information. He condemns what he does not understand and never makes progress because he thinks he knows it all. Such a man calls a follower of science and charts, a fool, but the follower of charts is a wise fool.

I quote from *Ist Corinthians 2:13-14*: "Which things also we speak, not in the words which man's wisdom teacheth, but which the Holy Ghost teacheth; comparing spiritual things with spiritual. But the natural man receiveth not the things of the spirit of God, for they are foolishness unto him, neither can he know them, because they are spiritually discerned."

The natural or average man considers science as applied to the stock market foolishness and condemns charts because he does not understand how to read them. To him they are foolishness because he does not know the rules by which to read them. He has not had years of experience and has not been trained to properly read or accurately determine the future course of stocks. The successful trader is the man who knows that he does not know it all and who is always trying to learn more. When once a man decides he knows it all about the stock market, he is doomed to failure. When activity decreases, stagnation sets in and when a man no longer continues to learn he goes backward, not forward. A successful man must have a plan and rules and follow them.

W. D. Gann, *Wall Street Stock Selector*

About Author

Sankar Srinivasan

National Stock Exchange of India's Certified Market Professional

Sankar Srinivasan is a Technical Analyst, living in Madurai City of Tamil Nadu State in India. He is having more than 10 years experience in Stocks, Fuures, Commodities and Currency Trading. He has conducted various training programs in Technical Analysis and Gann theories. He is s Certified Market Professional of National Stock Exchange of India

If you have any doubts, please contact me

Sankar Srinivasan

Petra.srini@gmail.com

Mobile/WhatsApp: +919042404390

MY OTHER BOOKS

GANN Square of 9

GANN MidPoint Theory

GANN Angle Theory

Fibonacci Retracement

www.ingramcontent.com/pod-product-compliance
Lightning Source LLC
Chambersburg PA
CBHW071014180526
45168CB00003B/1418